GIFTED & TALENTED®

*To develop
your child's gifts
and talents*

MATH
PUZZLES & GAMES

A Workbook for Ages 6–8

Written by Martha Cheney
Illustrated by Larry Nolte

LOWELL HOUSE JUVENILE

LOS ANGELES

CONTEMPORARY BOOKS

CHICAGO

Requests for such permissions should be addressed to:
Lowell House Juvenile
2020 Avenue of the Stars, Suite 300
Los Angeles, CA 90067

President and Publisher: Jack Artenstein
Director of Publishing Services: Rena Copperman
Editorial Director: Brenda Pope-Ostrow
Director of Art Production: Bret Perry
Editor: Linda Gorman
Designer: Treesha Runnells

Lowell House books can be purchased at special discounts when
ordered in bulk for premiums and special sales.
Please contact Customer Service at:
NTC/Contemporary
4255 W. Touhy Avenue
Lincolnwood, IL 60646
1-800-323-4900

Manufactured in the United States of America

ISBN: 1-56565-835-3

10   9   8   7   6   5   4   3   2   1

Note to Parents

GIFTED & TALENTED® WORKBOOKS will help develop your child's natural talents and gifts by providing activities to enhance critical and creative thinking skills. These skills of logic and reasoning teach children **how to think**. They are precisely the skills emphasized by teachers of gifted and talented children.

Thinking skills are the skills needed to be able to learn anything at any time. Unlike events, words, and teaching methods, thinking skills never change. If a child has a grasp of how to think, school success and even success in life will become more assured. In addition, the child will become self-confident as he or she approaches new tasks with the ability to think them through and discover solutions.

GIFTED & TALENTED® WORKBOOKS present these skills in a unique way, combining the basic subject areas of reading, language arts, and math with thinking skills. The top of each page is labeled to indicate the specific thinking skill developed. Here are some of the skills you will find:

- Deduction—the ability to reach a logical conclusion by interpreting clues

- Understanding Relationships—the ability to recognize how objects, shapes, and words are similar or dissimilar; to classify or categorize

- Sequencing—the ability to organize events, numbers; to recognize patterns

- Inference—the ability to reach a logical conclusion from given or assumed evidence

- Creative Thinking—the ability to generate unique ideas; to compare and contrast the same elements in different situations; to present imaginative solutions to problems

How to Use GIFTED & TALENTED® WORKBOOKS

Each book contains activities that challenge children. The activities range from easier to more difficult. You may need to work with your child on many of the pages, especially with the child who is a non-reader. However, even a non-reader can master thinking skills, and the sooner your child learns how to think, the better. Read the directions to your child and, if necessary, explain them. Let your child choose to do the activities that interest him or her. When interest wanes, stop. A page or two at a time may be enough, as the child should have fun while learning.

It is important to remember that these activities are designed to teach your child **how to think**, not how to find the right answer. Teachers of gifted children are never surprised when a child discovers a new "right" answer. For example, a child may be asked to choose the object that doesn't belong in this group: a table, a chair, a book, a desk. The best answer is **book**, since all the others are furniture. But a child could respond that all of them belong because they all could be found in an office or a library. The best way to react to this type of response is to praise the child and gently point out that there is another answer, too. While creativity should be encouraged, your child must look for the best and most **suitable** answer.

GIFTED & TALENTED® WORKBOOKS have been written by teachers. Educationally sound and endorsed by leaders in the gifted field, this series will benefit any child who demonstrates curiosity, imagination, a sense of fun and wonder about the world, and a desire to learn. These books will open your child's mind to new experiences and help fulfill his or her true potential.

Match the Circles

Look at this row of circles with patterns.

Which row of circles below exactly matches the row above?

Row _____ matches.

1.

2.

3.

4.

Match the Squares

Look at this row of squares with patterns.

Which row of squares below exactly matches the row above?

Row _____ matches.

1.

2.

3.

4.

Next in Line

What shape comes next in each pattern? Draw your answer on the line at the end of each row.

1.  _____

2.  _____

3.  _____

4.  _____

For an extra challenge: Create your own pattern of shapes. Ask a friend or a family member to figure out which shape comes next.

Fruit Salad

What number comes next in each pattern? Write your answer in the fruit at the end of each row.

2   4   6   8   10

5   10   15   20   25

11   22   33   44   55

1   2   1   3   1

0   3   0   5   0

Which fruit has the highest number? _____

Which fruit has the lowest number? _____

Play Ball!

What number comes next in each pattern? Write your answer in the ball at the end of each row.

1   10   100   1,000   10,000

95   90   85   80   75

24   26   25   27   26

12   23   34   45   56

1   3   6   8   11

Add the numbers in the baseball and the golf ball. What is the sum? _____

The Match Game

Draw a line from each shape inside the box to its matching shape outside the box. Do it as fast as you can. Ask a friend or a family member to time you.

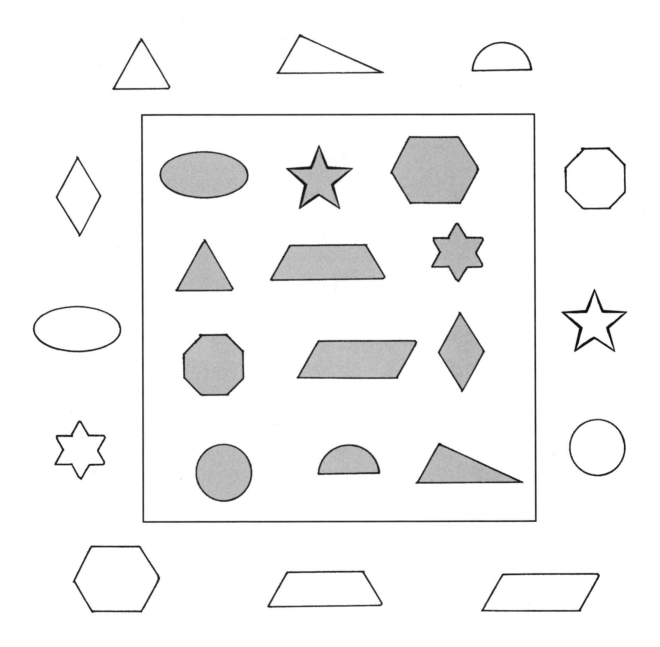

Add the Shapes

Each shape inside the box can be made by putting together two of the shapes outside the box. Draw a line from each shape inside the box to the two shapes that can be joined together to make it. Do it as fast as you can. Ask a friend or a family member to time you.

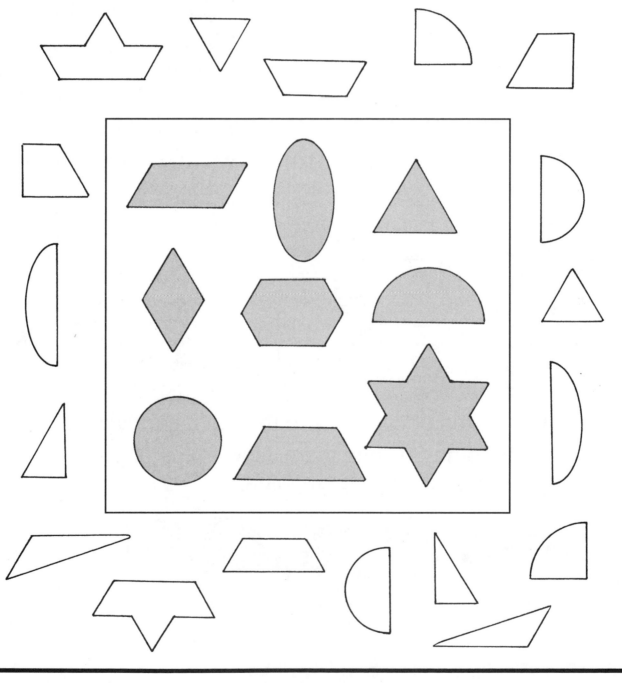

Most and Fewest

Which two bunches of bananas have the most bananas when you add them together? Circle them. How many bananas are in the two bunches altogether? _____

Which two stacks of books have the most books when you add them together? Circle them. How many books are in the two stacks altogether? _____

Which two boxes of candy have the most candy when you add them together? Circle them. How many pieces of candy are in the two boxes altogether? _____

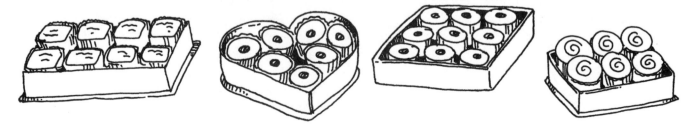

Which two nests have the fewest eggs when you add them together? Circle them. How many eggs are in the two nests altogether? _____

Which two bracelets have the fewest beads when you add them together? Circle them. How many beads do the two bracelets have altogether? _____

 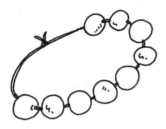 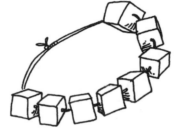 

Which two ladybugs have the fewest spots when you add them together? Circle them. How many spots do the two ladybugs have altogether? _____

Even and Odd

Even numbers are numbers that can be divided into two equal groups. **Odd numbers** are numbers that cannot be divided into two equal groups.

Decide whether each group below and on the next page contains an even number or an odd number of objects. Circle the correct answer.

Even   **Odd**   **Even**   **Odd**

Even   **Odd**   **Even**   **Odd**

Even   Odd   **Even   Odd**

Draw a picture of your whole family. Is the number of people in your family even or odd?

Find the Insects

Look at the chart of insects.

Match each insect below with one on the chart. Write the letter and number of each insect's box on the blank line. The first one has been done for you.

1. _B4_

2. _____

3. _____

4. _____

5. _____

6. _____

7. _____

8. _____

9. _____

10. _____

11. _____

12. _____

13. _____

14. _____

15. _____

16. _____

Juggling Numbers

These bears love to juggle apples—and numbers, too!

Fill in each apple with a number from 1 to 9. Use each number only once.

Make sure that the sum of the numbers on each bear's apples matches the number on that bear's hat.

Find the Vehicles

Look at the chart of vehicles.

Match each vehicle below with one on the chart. Write the letter and number of each vehicle's box on the blank line. The first one has been done for you.

1. _A4_

2. _____

3. _____

4. _____

5. _____

6. _____

7. _____

8. _____

9. _____

10. _____

11. _____

12. _____

13. _____

14. _____

15. _____

16. _____

Hop and Add

Webster the frog likes to play a game with the lily pads in his pond. Each lily pad has a number. As he hops from pad to pad, Webster adds the numbers along his path until he is back home again.

Find at least two paths for Webster that add up to 17.

Find at least one path that adds up to 22.

Find at least one path that adds up to 20.

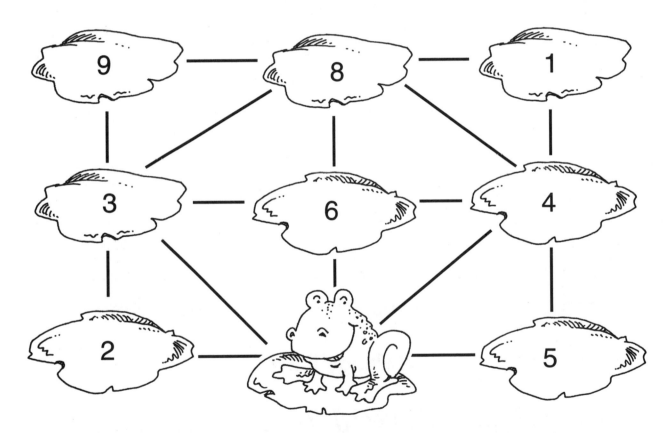

Choose any other number. Can you find a path that equals that number?

The Shell Collection

Peggy went to the beach and collected lots of seashells.

Match each shell Peggy found with
the shells on the graph below.
Color in one space in the correct
row for each of the shells
she found.

	1	2	3	4	5	6	7	8

Use the graph to help you answer these questions.

How many _____ did Peggy find? _____

How many _____ did Peggy find? _____

How many _____ and _____ did Peggy find altogether?

_____

The Shape Store

At the shape store, each item is priced according to the shapes that it is made of. Each shape has a different price.

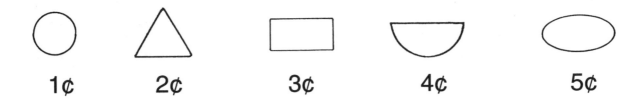

1¢   2¢   3¢   4¢   5¢

How much do the toys below cost? To find out, count the different shapes that make up each toy and figure out how much each shape costs. For example, the three triangles on the boat cost 6¢ (2¢ + 2¢ + 2¢).

For each toy, add the prices of all the shapes to get the total amount. Fill in each tag with the correct price.

Dot to Dot

Count by twos to connect the dots and complete the picture.
Before you begin, can you guess what the picture will be?

1, 2, 3—Follow Me!

Consecutive numbers are numbers that follow each other in order. For example, 4, 5, and 6 are consecutive numbers.

Which two consecutive numbers add up to 21?

_____ _____

Which three consecutive numbers
add up to 21?

_____ _____ _____

Which three consecutive
numbers add up to 30?

_____ _____ _____

Which four consecutive numbers add up to 30?

_____ _____ _____ _____

Favorite Numbers

Jack and Tammy each have a favorite number. Use the clues they have given you to find their numbers.

Hint: Even numbers can be divided into two equal parts. Odd numbers cannot be divided into two equal parts.

My number is odd.

My number is one greater than Tammy's number.

Our numbers added together equal less than 10.

My number is even.

My number is greater than 2.

Our numbers added together equal more than 5.

Jack's favorite number is _____.

Tammy's favorite number is _____.

What is your favorite number? _____ Make up a set of clues that describe your favorite number.

Where's Rudy?

Rudy is the best football player on the team. Read the clues to find Rudy. Draw a circle around him.

Rudy's jersey number is greater than 10.

Rudy's jersey number is made up of two different numbers.

Rudy's jersey number is less than 20.

Rudy's jersey number is not an odd number.

Rhonda's Roses

Rhonda is making bouquets of yellow roses and red roses. There are seven roses in each bouquet. She wants at least one yellow rose and one red rose in each bouquet.

Color each bouquet to show the different number combinations of yellow roses and red roses that Rhonda might use. Make each bouquet different from the others.

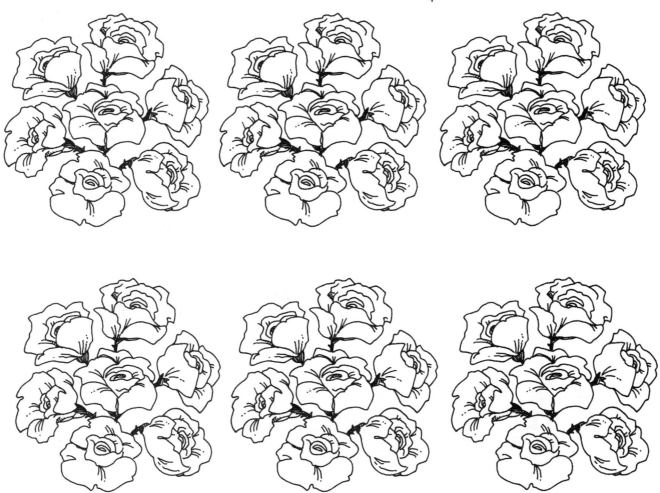

Larry the Logger

Larry the logger needs to move these logs. He can only move one log at a time because they are so heavy. He cannot move any log that is covered by part of another log.

Number the logs in the order that Larry can move them.

Leapfrog

The frogs below are supposed to be lined up according to their numbers, from smallest to largest. But some frogs are out of order!

Draw a line to connect the two frogs in each row that must switch places so that the numbers are in the correct order.

Number Puzzle

On the number grid below, draw a red line through the three numbers that add up to 16.

Draw a blue line through the three numbers that add up to 13.

9   2   4

5   1   7

8   3   6

On the number grid below, draw a red line through the three numbers that give you the highest total. What is the total? _____

Draw a blue line through the three numbers that give you the lowest total. What is the total? _____

9   2   4

5   1   7

8   3   6

What's the Weight?

When you make an **estimate,** you try to guess an amount. Draw a line from each object on the left to its possible weight on the right.

1 pound

500 pounds

40 pounds

15 pounds

200 pounds

For an extra challenge: Which two objects together weigh 16 pounds? _____

Which two objects together weigh 240 pounds?

_____

How Tall?

When you make an **estimate,** you try to guess an amount. Draw a line from each object on the left to its possible height on the right.

15 feet

4 feet

1 foot

25 feet

10 feet

For an extra challenge: If the girl stood on the elephant's back, would she be taller or shorter than the giraffe?

_____

How much taller or shorter? _____

Find Ted's Meal

Ted went to his favorite restaurant to eat. Here are some of the foods that were on the menu.

Grilled cheese sandwich $3

Hamburger $3

French fries $2

Soup $2

Salad $1

Milk $1

Ted spent $5. What did he order? Circle Ted's meal below.

Maggie's Mouse

Maggie bought a mouse for $1. She paid for it using a combination of nickels, dimes, and quarters.

Fill in the chart below to show four different combinations of coins Maggie might have used to pay for the mouse.

5¢	10¢	25¢	Total
			$1.00
			$1.00
			$1.00
			$1.00

Number Grid

Use the clues to fill in the boxes with the numbers 1 to 9.
Use each number only once.

A1: This number is even.
A2: This number is the sum of 3 + 4.
A3: This number is half of 10.

B1: This number is one less than A3.
B2: This number is one greater than C2.
B3: This number is the same as half a dozen.

C1: This number is odd.
C2: This number is half of B1.
C3: This number is one greater than A1.

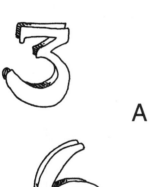

	1	2	3
A			
B			
C			

Dot to Dot

Count by fives to connect the dots and complete the picture.
Before you begin, can you guess what the picture will be?

Search for 16

Draw a circle around each group of numbers whose sum equals 16. The numbers must be in a straight line, either up and down or across. One group is circled for you.

Hint: There may be two, three, or four numbers in a group!

5 4 3 2 6 8

7 1 8 9 5 2

2 9 4 7 1 3

2 6 1 8 8 5

Search for 21

Draw a circle around each group of numbers whose sum equals 21. The numbers must be in a straight line, either up and down or across. One group is circled for you.

Hint: There may be three, four, or five numbers in a group!

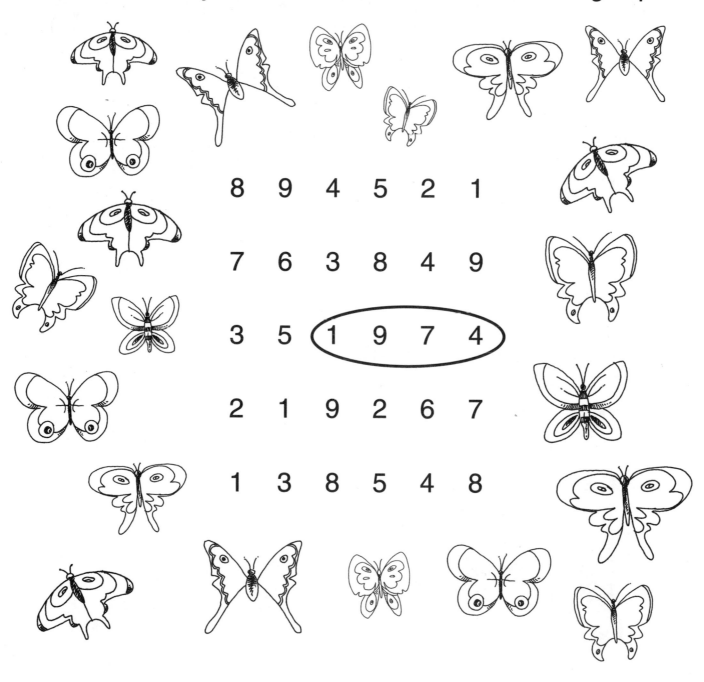

8 9 4 5 2 1

7 6 3 8 4 9

3 5 (1 9 7 4)

2 1 9 2 6 7

1 3 8 5 4 8

At the Zoo

Look at the graph below. It tells how many animals of each kind the Clark City Zoo has.

	1	2	3	4	5	6	7
lions	▓	▓	▓	▓	▓		
elephants	▓	▓	▓				
gorillas	▓	▓	▓				
zebras	▓	▓	▓	▓	▓	▓	▓
giraffes	▓	▓	▓	▓	▓		

Use the information on the graph to decide if each statement below is true (**T**) or false (**F**).

1. There are more lions than zebras.   **T**   **F**
2. The are fewer elephants than giraffes.   **T**   **F**
3. The number of gorillas and lions altogether is an odd number.   **T**   **F**
4. The number of zebras and elephants altogether is an even number.   **T**   **F**

Home from School

Look at the graph below. It tells how many days of school each of the children in the Young family missed last year.

	1	2	3	4	5	6	7
Sally	▓	▓	▓				
Jack	▓	▓	▓	▓	▓	▓	
Bennett	▓	▓	▓				
Annie	▓	▓	▓	▓	▓		

Use the information on the graph to decide if each statement below is true (**T**) or false (**F**).

1. The boys missed more days of school than the girls. **T**   **F**

2. Sally and Bennett missed the same number of days. **T**   **F**

3. Altogether, Jack and Annie missed more than 12 days. **T**   **F**

4. Altogether, the children missed 15 days. **T**   **F**

Road Signs

Solve the problems below using multiplication. The pictures will help you.

How many sides are there on four yield signs? _____

(Add your answer from above to the answer
to the next problem. Write the total next to
the equals sign.)
How many sides are there on two stop signs?　+ _____

(Subtract your answer to the next problem
from the total above. Write your answer next to
the equals sign.)
How many sides are there on five right-turn
signs?　－ _____

　＝ _____

Circle the truck that shows the correct answer.

All About Animals

Solve the problems below using multiplication. The pictures will help you.

How many legs do ten horses have? _____

(Add your answer from above to the answer to the next problem. Write the total next to the equals sign.)

How many tusks do seven elephants have?   + _____

(Subtract your answer to the next problem from the total above. Write your answer next to the equals sign.)

How many legs do four spiders have?   − _____

= _____

Circle the penguin that shows the correct answer.

A Math Competition

Fire Creek School had a math competition. Use the clues below to determine which students won first, second, and third place.

The winner solved 20 problems correctly.

Shannon solved 16 problems correctly.

Rusty solved more problems than Shannon.

Conrad was not the winner.

One student solved 18 problems.

Write the names of the winners on the ribbons they won.

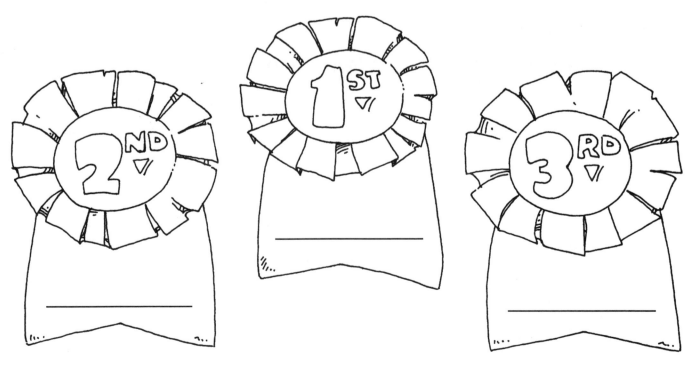

Secret Number

What secret number is the spy carrying? Read the clues to find out. Each clue will help you eliminate one or more numbers on the grid. Place an **X** on each number that you eliminate.

This number does not have a 2 in the ones place.

This number is odd.

This number is greater than 59.

The first and second digits of this number are the same.

This number does not have a 9 in the tens place.

What is the secret number? _____

1	2	3	4	5	6	7	8	9	10
11	12	13	14	15	16	17	18	19	20
21	22	23	24	25	26	27	28	29	30
31	32	33	34	35	36	37	38	39	40
41	42	43	44	45	46	47	48	49	50
51	52	53	54	55	56	57	58	59	60
61	62	63	64	65	66	67	68	69	70
71	72	73	74	75	76	77	78	79	80
81	82	83	84	85	86	87	88	89	90
91	92	93	94	95	96	97	98	99	100

A Perfect Day for a Picnic

Cindy wants all her friends to join her for a picnic. Use the information Cindy has gathered to help her decide which day will be best.

Lisa will be out of town for two weeks beginning on the 14th.

It is supposed to rain on the first weekend of the month.

Ross has to work every day except Saturday and Sunday.

Ted can't come on Sunday because he goes to church.

Which day should Cindy choose for her picnic? _____

S	M	T	W	Th	F	S
	1	2	3	4	5	6
7	8	9	10	11	12	13
14	15	16	17	18	19	20
21	22	23	24	25	26	27
28	29	30				

JUNE

It's a Date!

Nina is making plans for the month of July. Help her by writing down the date for each of the events listed below.

She is going to a concert on the first Friday of the month.
The date is July _____.

Her family is going to see the circus on the third Saturday of the month.
The date is July _____.

She is going to a friend's birthday party on the second Tuesday of the month.
The date is July _____.

Her grandparents are coming to visit on the fourth Sunday of the month.
The date is July _____.

		JULY				
S	M	T	W	Th	F	S
			1	2	3	4
5	6	7	8	9	10	11
12	13	14	15	16	17	18
19	20	21	22	23	24	25
26	27	28	29	30	31	

Hippity Hop!

The rabbits below are supposed to be lined up according to their numbers, from smallest to largest. But some rabbits are out of order!

Draw a line to connect the two rabbits in each row that must switch places so that the numbers are in the correct order.

Secret Number

What secret number is the pirate looking for? Read the clues to find out. Each clue will help you eliminate one or more numbers on the grid. Place an **X** on each number that you eliminate.

This number is even.

The digits of this number can be added together to make a total that is greater than 9.

This number does not have a 5 in the tens place.

When the smaller digit in this number is subtracted from the larger digit, the answer is 5.

The first digit of this number is larger than the second digit.

What is the secret number? _____

1	2	3	4	5	6	7	8	9	10
11	12	13	14	15	16	17	18	19	20
21	22	23	24	25	26	27	28	29	30
31	32	33	34	35	36	37	38	39	40
41	42	43	44	45	46	47	48	49	50
51	52	53	54	55	56	57	58	59	60
61	62	63	64	65	66	67	68	69	70
71	72	73	74	75	76	77	78	79	80
81	82	83	84	85	86	87	88	89	90
91	92	93	94	95	96	97	98	99	100

Time for School

Molly got up at 7 o'clock. She went to school at 8:30. At 9 o'clock she had a math class. After that, she had a science lesson. At 12 o'clock she ate lunch. After lunch, she had social studies. At 2:30 she had an art lesson. At 3:30 Molly went home.

The clocks below show the times for each of the events in Molly's day. Number the clocks in order from 1 to 8. On the blank line below each clock, write what Molly did at that time. The first one is done for you.

8			

went home

Number Crossword

Answer the questions below to solve the crossword puzzle. For each answer, spell out the number, putting one letter in each box.

Across

1. How many tens are there in 100?

4. How much is half a dozen?

5. What is the loneliest number?

7. How many bears did Goldilocks meet?

8. How many innings are in a baseball game?

9. How many toes do you have on each foot?

Down

2. How many pints are in a gallon?

3. How many seasons are in a year?

4. How many dwarfs did Snow White meet?

6. How many months are in a year?

The Wild West

The stagecoach that travels through the Old West towns on this map has a new driver, Dusty McGee.

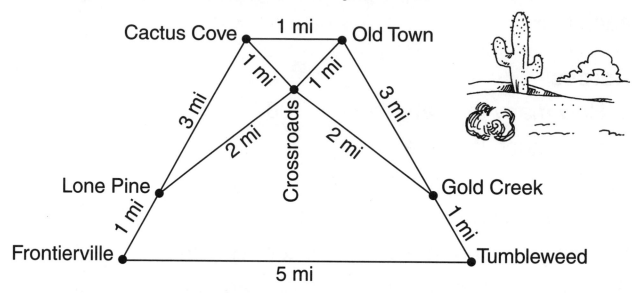

Help Dusty find the shortest route between Lone Pine and Tumbleweed.

How many miles long is this route? _____ What towns will he stop in along the way? _____

What route should Dusty take from Tumbleweed back to Lone Pine if he has passengers to pick up in Cactus Cove and Crossroads? Using a crayon, trace Dusty's route on the map. How many miles long is this route? _____

Secret Number

What secret number is the thief trying to steal? Read the clues to find out. Each clue will help you eliminate one or more numbers on the grid. Place an **X** on each number that you eliminate.

This number has two digits.

This number does not contain a zero.

This number is an even number.

The digits of this number make an odd number when added together.

The digit in the tens place is larger than the digit in the ones place.

The number is less than 50.

What is the secret number? _____

1	2	3	4	5	6	7	8	9	10
11	12	13	14	15	16	17	18	19	20
21	22	23	24	25	26	27	28	29	30
31	32	33	34	35	36	37	38	39	40
41	42	43	44	45	46	47	48	49	50
51	52	53	54	55	56	57	58	59	60
61	62	63	64	65	66	67	68	69	70
71	72	73	74	75	76	77	78	79	80
81	82	83	84	85	86	87	88	89	90
91	92	93	94	95	96	97	98	99	100

A Lost Little Monster

Manfred the Monster is lost! Help Manfred find his way home. Draw a path through the numbers to the answer next to Manfred's cave.

Move from a number to a plus or a minus sign, then to another number. You can move up, down, or across, but not diagonally.

Hint: There may be more than one path that leads to the answer!

START

6	+	2	–	5	+
–		4	–	3	–	7
1	+	3	+	2	+
–		2	+	6	–	4
5	–	1	+	3	–
+		2	–	4	+	5 = 10

A Honey of a Maze

Follow Buzzy Bee back to the hive, and maybe he'll share his honey with you! Draw a path through the numbers to the answer next to the hive.

Move from a number to a plus or a minus sign, then to another number. You can move up, down, or across, but not diagonally.

Hint: There may be more than one path that leads to the answer!

 START

3	–	5	+	2	–
+	4	–	1	+	6
2	–	3	+	4	–
+	1	–	5	–	1
3	–	4	+	2	–
+	6	–	3	+	4 = 9

The Bean Game

You will need about 100 dried beans (or other small counting objects) for this activity.

Solve this problem: 1 x 10 = ?
Place 1 bean in each of the 10 circles on this page and the next.
How many beans are there altogether? _____

Solve this problem: 2 x 4 = ?
Place 2 beans in 4 circles.
How many beans are there altogether? _____

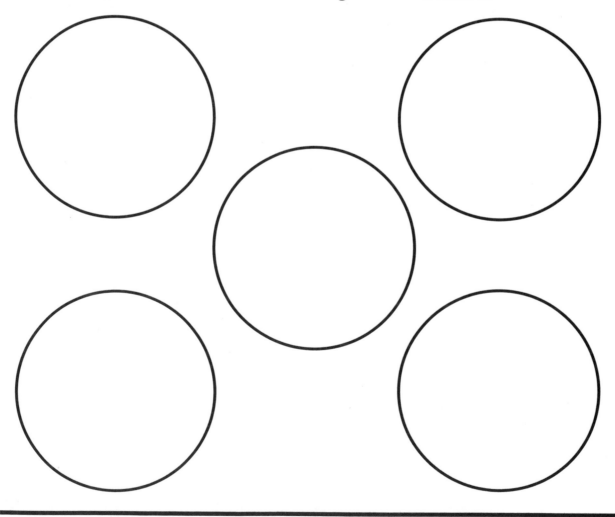

Use the beans to find the answers to these problems.

3 x 5 = _____   4 x 4 = _____

4 x 8 = _____   3 x 8 = _____

6 x 2 = _____   7 x 9 = _____

7 x 7 = _____   6 x 7 = _____

5 x 9 = _____   5 x 8 = _____

9 x 9 = _____   3 x 4 = _____

7 x 6 = _____   6 x 10 = _____

Make up problems of your own to solve.

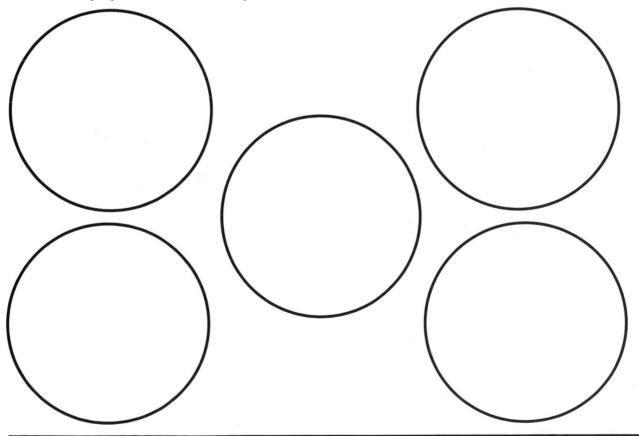

Pizza Pies

Gina ordered a cheese pizza. She cut the pizza into eight slices and ate three slices. Draw lines through the pizza below to make eight equal slices. Then color in three slices to show how much Gina ate.

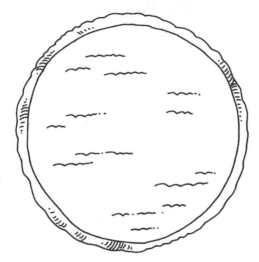

Robbie ordered a pepperoni pizza. He cut the pizza into four slices and ate two slices. Draw lines through the pizza below to make four equal slices. Then color in two slices to show how much Robbie ate.

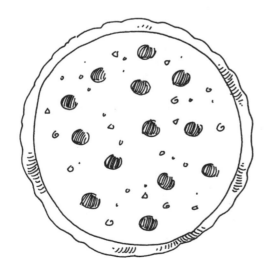

Who ate more pizza, Gina or Robbie? _____

A Secret Code

Here is a secret code for you to learn. Fill in the missing code for numbers 7 and 9.

Write the following numbers in code. The first one is done for you.

24 ●● △

63 _____

99 _____

157 _____

208 _____

431 _____

What does your phone number look like in secret code? Write it here. _____

Which Witch Is Which?

Nelda, Hilda, and Frieda are three friendly witches. Each witch rides on a different colored broom. Their ages are 150, 100, and 200. Use the clues to find out each witch's age and the color of her broom.

The witch who rides the blue broom is twice as old as the witch who rides the red broom.

Hilda is 50 years younger than the witch who rides the green broom.

Frieda's age does not have an even number in it.

Witch	Age	Color of Broom

Cookie Time

Adam, Andrew, and Daniel are brothers. One brother is 10 years old, one is 8, and one is 12. Each boy has a favorite cookie. Use the clues below to find out each boy's age and favorite kind of cookie.

The boy who likes chocolate chip cookies is the youngest.

Adam is older than Daniel.

The boy who likes peanut butter cookies is older than the boy who likes molasses cookies.

Andrew is not the youngest.

Adam does not like molasses cookies.

Name	Age	Favorite Cookie

X's and 0's

This game is just like regular tic-tac-toe except that a player must place five X's or 0's in a row in order to win the game. The row may run up and down, across, or diagonally.

Here are some sample games.

It is X's turn. Where should he place his mark?

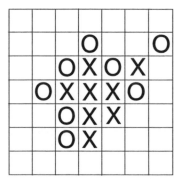

It is 0's turn. Where should she place her mark?

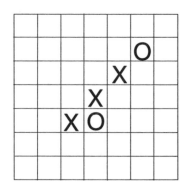

Ask a friend or a family member to play, or try it by yourself. You can make more game boards like these on separate sheets of paper.

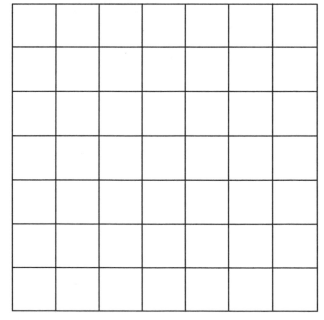

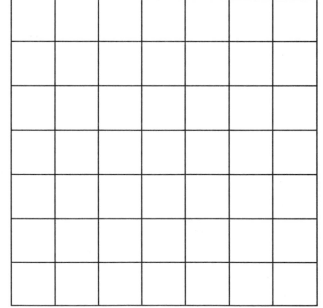

Answers

Page 5
Row 2 matches.

Page 6
Row 4 matches.

Page 7
1.   2.   3.   4.

Page 8
pineapple – 12
lemon – 30
apple – 66
banana – 4
strawberry – 7
highest number: apple
lowest number: banana

Page 9
football – 100,000
bowling ball – 70
baseball – 28
basketball – 67
golf ball – 13
baseball + golf ball = 41

Page 10
Lines should be drawn to connect the following shapes:

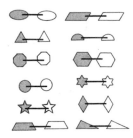

Page 11

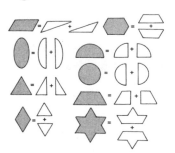

Pages 12–13

11 bananas altogether

15 books altogether

17 pieces altogether

9 eggs altogether

11 beads altogether

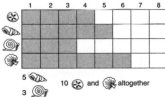

9 spots altogether

Pages 14–15
6 fish – Even
9 hats – Odd
13 flowers – Odd
14 spiders – Even
5 pumpkins – Odd
10 boots and shoes – Even
Rest of answer will vary.

Page 16
2. B3	7. A1	12. C4
3. B1	8. D1	13. A4
4. D4	9. C3	14. D3
5. B2	10. A2	15. C2
6. A3	11. D2	16. C1

Page 17
Bear wearing hat 13 is juggling apples 2, 4, and 7.
Bear wearing hat 14 is juggling apples 3, 5, and 6.
Bear wearing hat 18 is juggling apples 1, 8, and 9.

Page 18
2. B4	7. B2	12. A1
3. C2	8. B3	13. D2
4. D1	9. A2	14. A3
5. C1	10. C4	15. C3
6. B1	11. D4	16. D3

Page 19

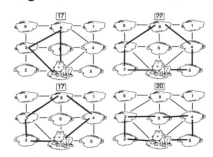

Page 20

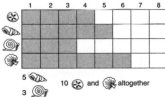

5 🐌 snails
3 🐌

10 🐚 and 🐚 altogether

Page 21
Bear:	3 half-circles = 12¢
	5 circles = 5¢
	2 triangles = 4¢
	4 ovals = 20¢
	Total cost = 41¢
Doll:	14 circles = 14¢
	4 triangles = 8¢
	3 half-circles = 12¢
	5 rectangles = 15¢
	4 ovals = 20¢
	Total cost = 69¢
Boat:	3 triangles = 6¢
	2 rectangles = 6¢
	5 circles = 5¢
	Total cost = 17¢

Page 22

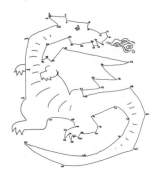

Page 23
21 = 10 + 11
21 = 6 + 7 + 8
30 = 9 + 10 + 11
30 = 6 + 7 + 8 + 9

Page 24
Jack's favorite number is 5.
Tammy's favorite number is 4.
Rest of answer will vary.

Page 25
Rudy is number 14.

Page 26
Color combinations for
each bouquet:

Yellow roses	Red roses
1	6
2	5
3	4
4	3
5	2
6	1

Page 27

Page 28
The frogs with these numbers
must switch places:
21 and 19
34 and 26
84 and 81
41 and 36
90 and 87

Page 29

Page 30
dog – 40 pounds
rat – 1 pound
bear – 200 pounds
baby – 15 pounds
piano – 500 pounds
Extra challenge: Rat and baby
weigh 16 pounds altogether.
Dog and bear weigh 240 pounds
altogether.

Page 31
girl – 4 feet
elephant – 10 feet
footstool – 1 foot
barn – 25 feet
giraffe – 15 feet
Extra challenge: Shorter by 1 foot.

Page 32

Page 33
Sample combinations:

Nickels	Dimes	Quarters
1	2	3
2	4	2
3	1	3
4	3	2
5	5	1
6	2	2

Page 34

	1	2	3
A	8	7	5
B	4	3	6
C	1	2	9

Page 35

Page 36

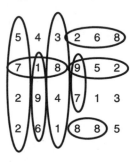

Page 37

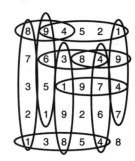

Page 38
1. F
2. T
3. F
4. F

Page 39
1. T
2. T
3. F
4. F

Page 40
yield signs: 4 x 3 sides = 12
stop signs: 2 x 8 sides = 16
12 + 16 = 28
right-turn signs: 5 x 4 sides = 20
28 - 20 = 8
Circle the truck with the number 8.

Page 41

horses: 10 x 4 legs = 40
elephants: 7 x 2 tusks = 14
40 + 14 = 54
spiders: 4 x 8 legs = 32
54 - 32 = 22
Circle the penguin with the number 22.

Page 42

1st – Rusty
2nd – Conrad
3rd – Shannon

Page 43

The secret number is 77.

Page 44

June 13

Page 45

first Friday – July 3
third Saturday – July 18
second Tuesday – July 14
fourth Sunday – July 26

Page 46

The rabbits with these numbers must switch places:
112 and 106
386 and 311
734 and 529
577 and 318
525 and 475

Page 47

The secret number is 94.

Page 48

went home   got up
math class   went to school
had lunch   art lesson
social studies science lesson

Page 49

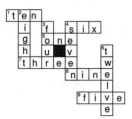

Page 50

5 miles
Crossroads and Gold Creek

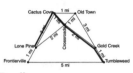

7 miles

Page 51

The secret number is 32.

Page 52

Sample answer:

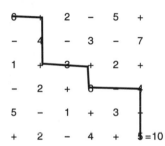

Page 53

Sample answer:

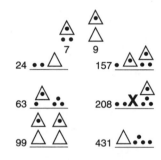

Pages 54–55

1 x 10 = 10	2 x 4 = 8
3 x 5 = 15	4 x 4 = 16
4 x 8 = 32	3 x 8 = 24
6 x 2 = 12	7 x 9 = 63
7 x 7 = 49	6 x 7 = 42
5 x 9 = 45	5 x 8 = 40
9 x 9 = 81	3 x 4 = 12
7 x 6 = 42	6 x 10 = 60

Page 56

Robbie ate more pizza.

Page 57

24 ••△   157 △△••
7   9
63 △ • •   208 ✗ • •
99 △ △   431 △ • • •

Rest of answer will vary.

Page 58

Witch	Age	Color of Broom
Hilda	100	red
Frieda	150	green
Nelda	200	blue

Page 59

Name	Age	Favorite Cookie
Daniel	8	chocolate chip
Andrew	10	molasses
Adam	12	peanut butter

Page 60